i Hope
for Heaven

Jennifer Ingram

Trilogy Christian Publishers

A Wholly Owned Subsidiary of Trinity Broadcasting Network

2442 Michelle Drive

Tustin, CA 92780

Copyright © 2022 Jennifer Ingram

All Scripture quotations, unless otherwise noted, taken from THE HOLY BIBLE, NEW INTERNATIONAL VERSION®, NIV® Copyright © 1973, 1978, 1984, 2011 by Biblica, Inc.® Used by permission. All rights reserved worldwide.

Scripture quotations marked (KJV) taken from *The Holy Bible, King James Version*. Cambridge Edition: 1769.

All rights reserved, including the right to reproduce this book or portions thereof in any form whatsoever.

For information, address Trilogy Christian Publishing

Rights Department, 2442 Michelle Drive, Tustin, Ca 92780.

Trilogy Christian Publishing/TBN and colophon are trademarks of Trinity Broadcasting Network.

For information about special discounts for bulk purchases, please contact Trilogy Christian Publishing.

Manufactured in the United States of America

Trilogy Disclaimer: The views and content expressed in this book are those of the author and may not necessarily reflect the views and doctrine of Trilogy Christian Publishing or the Trinity Broadcasting Network.

10 9 8 7 6 5 4 3 2 1

Library of Congress Cataloging-in-Publication Data is available.

ISBN 978-1-68556-873-3

ISBN 978-1-68556-874-0 (ebook)

Dedication

To my Lord and Savior Jesus Christ, who comforted me and showed me His character through my grief. May this work be pleasing to You and may Your light shine through me.

To my precious husband, Chad, who has stood by me when things were so unpleasant. Thank you for giving me the courage I didn't think I had and for helping me believe in myself.

To my children who are gifts from God: Camden, Savannah, and Bristol. May my words open your eyes to see me in a different light and give you insight into your mother's grief and healing. May this book grow you in your faith in Jesus as a representative of Peyton's family.

Table of Contents

Preface	7
Introduction	9
In the Beginning	11
A Mom's Worst Nightmare	17
Starting a Life Without Peyton	27
God Steps In	37
Camden's Gifts	43
A New Family	53
Trapped in Grief	63
Finally, Complete Healing	67
Journal Entries	77
"On Peyton's Grave" by Jennifer Ingram	85
How to Help Someone Who Is Grieving	87
Yielding to Emergency Vehicles	89
Confirmations and Dates	90

Hope - Confidence in a future event[1].
Heaven - God's dwelling place[2].

Now the God of hope fill you with all joy and peace in believing, that ye may abound in hope, through the power of the Holy Ghost.
                              Romans 15:13 (KJV)

---

1   *Webster's 1828 Dictionary*, s.v. "Hope (*noun*)," 1828, https://www.kingjamesbibledictionary.com/Dictionary/hope.
2   *Webster's 1828 Dictionary*, s.v. "Heaven (*noun*)," 1828, https://kingjamesbibledictionary.com/Dictionary/heavens.

Preface

This story comes from a grieving mom's heart in search of hope. I want to share my incredible story with my loved ones and friends who have supported me through this long journey. In this novel, maybe my three children still on this earth will understand all that we went through as a family. I want them to know how much I love them and to experience this journey with me as me as the author. For several years, I know I could not give myself completely to them because of what happened to their brother. I also want to share my hope with other moms who like me have lost a child.

There are many things that I have debated sharing in this book, many things that others might not believe or question. But I want to share my whole story, no pieces left out. I know that those around me who witnessed these things know it is true. I believe God allowed these things to happen not just to bring me hope and comfort but also so I could share them with you.

The first year after Peyton died, I experienced an amazing, intimate walk with the Lord. He felt closer to me than He ever had. I believe God allowed me to see His character. I felt the presence of the Lord just as I would if He were physically standing next to me. When I say I heard God speak to me, it was not in audible voice. It was a strong voice that spoke to my spirit. Most of my experiences that I am going to share with you were always backed up by something or someone confirming it. I was dedicated to writing in my journal and documented dates with all of my experiences. Looking back, it encouraged me to see how far I have come. Most of my experiences that happened during this time were no surprise to me. As I go back rereading and remembering the things that happened, I am astonished also in awe at how the Lord creatively and lovingly comforted me as my earthly father would. My eyes and my heart were open to whatever God had to tell me or show me in order for me to heal; I knew He had a plan and purpose for allowing my son to go to heaven.

Introduction

I began writing my story after Peyton died. I journaled thoughts and miracles God was showing me. I never meant to write a book in the beginning, yet as I began to tell my stories, everyone's words were the same, you have to write a book. I had a vision and God showed me the name of my book, "i hope for Heaven". I had yet to put much time in writing it and at this stage it was mostly an idea. As the years ticked by, I began the editing process and decided for myself that the lower case "i" wouldn't make sense to others. One evening, a dinner date was set for me to meet a mom who had lost her son to murder. A friend set up this date because this other mom had written a book about her journey through grief, and my friend knew she could help me with my book process. Upon meeting and discussing my book, she asked the name of my book. When I told her it was "I hope for Heaven", she immediately said, "It's with a little "I," right?" I broke down because her question was the confirmation I needed for the title. She even took a piece of paper and wrote what she saw in her mind's eye, which was the exact same way God had shown me the title years before.

This process has taken me years, fifteen to be exact. I always had a burning in my spirit to finish this book and felt as Paul says in 1 Corinthians 9:16, Woe is me if I don't speak the gospel. I have kept a fire in my spirit to finish this book. I have had visions of my book from God. I carried that with me, knowing this was God's path for my grief. The process has been a long journey until this point because God had so much to teach me through my years of hurt. The timing just was never right to publish until now.

Through my brokenness over the death of my son, Peyton, I was stripped of everything I once believed: these preconceived notions of how I believed God was supposed to be. I was stripped of everyone's opinion, view, and interpretation of who they believed God to be. I had to find out who God was for myself and myself alone. I had to build my own truth. A truth that has had to be understood and relearned through each season of my life. This story is not just about my first stages of grief but also years of living and learning to adapt my grief into my life and through God's filter. This is my story of how I found God in the midst of raw and ultimate brokenness.

Chapter 1

In the Beginning

For I know the thoughts that I think toward you, saith the Lord, thoughts of peace, and not evil to give you an expected end.
Jeremiah 29:11 (KJV)

I had a pretty normal childhood. I was born three years after my sister, Gena, to two of the most wonderful parents in the world. My mother says her only dream and purpose in life was to be a mom. I had a home filled with love, support, and laughter. As childhood goes, mine was picture perfect; I was blessed beyond measure. As I grew up, no big changes happened in my life. My life had a very stable, routine, and I was surrounded by friends and a loving family. I loved school and was a social butterfly. I have always had an easy-going, type B personality.

When I entered middle school, we moved out of my childhood home and into a beautiful house my daddy had built himself. Little did my father know that he was moving his daughters into the neighborhood of their future husbands. My sister soon fell in love with the star quarterback across the street. She would date him all through high school, and he would become my brother-in-law a few years after they graduated. I met my soon-to-be husband, Chad Ingram, when we rode the bus together to middle school. We became instant friends. In the future I would compare each boy I dated to Chad because he treated me so well. Chad remained my best friend for many years, up until college. Then, one day, the Lord revealed to me that he was "the one."

On February 2, 1997, Chad and I were married. Marriage was wonderful but brought on many new challenges. During the first few years of our marriage, learning to communicate productively was a struggle, a struggle we still face. Our problems escalated until we separated in the year 2000. We thought divorce was a solution, but through God, we were able to reconcile. It took a lot of work on both of our parts. I feel that because we had such a strong foundation of friendship, we survived through those extremely difficult times. Also, I feel we had to endure hardships in our marriage in order to learn how to communicate to keep us together through the most grueling times in our lives.

After being married for six years we both decided it was time for children. Not too long after this decision we were pregnant with our first child. I had a wonderful pregnancy and loved every moment of being pregnant. On February 7, 2003, Steven Peyton was welcomed into this world. My grandmother loved the name Peyton and we wanted her to get to name one of her great-grandchildren. Peyton entered this world healthy, seven pounds and seven ounces.

After delivering Peyton, I could not pass my placenta because it was attached to my uterine wall, a condition known as placenta accreta. God had had already orchestrated the detail of giving me this particular OBGYN because, even with my rare condition, he had just experienced another patient whom upon delivery had the same condition. He had done research and was prepared for what was to come. He explained that he was going to try to free my placenta by pulling it loose by hand. If he could not, he would have to do an emergency hysterectomy. Also, if he did pull it loose there was a possibility part of the placenta could be left behind leaving my body still to respond like I was pregnant, pumping blood inside of me. Again, if this occurred, I could be rushed into emergency surgery with the extreme possibility that I could hemorrhage and possibly die.

In the Beginning

My doctor pulled and tugged for about an hour until the placenta was pulled from my uterus. I had lost a lot of blood but was doing good. I would find out later that most doctors given this same rare situation would have given me a hysterectomy. But because my doctor had just had an experience like mine, he knew what to do. Peyton could have been my only child but my God intervened.

Peyton was born with a head full of strawberry blond hair that stood straight up. He was the most beautiful baby I had ever laid my eyes on. I was instantly in love. As far as babies go, he was perfect. Now, two became three; we were finally a family.

Peyton was always smiling, always laughing. He was a wonderful baby, but as he grew older, he became more of a challenge. He was always getting into everything. I couldn't leave him alone for a second. He always got into mischief and got into it quickly. He was not a bad child, just stuffed with the energy and curiosity of 10 children. I never got to sit down and I thought this was just the normal child. I was always told, "Wow, that boy is into EVERYTHING!" *That's the way all toddlers are, right?* I thought.

Five days before Peyton turned two, we had his baby brother Camden "Camey" Wayne. Peyton could not have been happier. He loved his "brudder," as he called him, to pieces. Now my busy eldest son had a baby to take care of. He took on responsibilities, a little too much at times. When Camden was only a couple of months old, I caught Peyton carrying him around. When Camden was a bit older, I found him sitting up and was so excited to see him learning how to sit only to find out, his big brother would sit him up. I could not leave the two alone for a millisecond. Peyton thought it was funny to push Camey over when he was learning to sit. He thought it even funnier to steal his pacifier and run and hide with it.

As Camden grew, so the bond between the brothers grew. I would catch them rolling on the floor together and rush to "save" Camden only to find him with a huge smile probably the one who started the wrestling. He quickly learned how to be a rough, tough, and mischievous little boy all thanks to his big brother of course.

Not only did the two learn to play well together, they learned to fight well together too. I now had "referee" on my resume. Peyton would mostly keep his little brother out of trouble (off the stairs, out of the toilet, etc.) unless it looked fun to Peyton. Then he would join in the fun only to blame it on his little "brudder" when they were caught. The two were joined at the hip. I never had a moment's peace. When Camden woke up from his naps, Peyton loved to run upstairs by himself close the door behind him and sing *Twinkle, Twinkle Little Star* to Camden. He would then climb in his baby bed, and they would wrestle. This match would be followed by a yell for the okay to enter the room.

At one point Camden started jumping out of his baby bed. I could never figure out how he would get out. One morning, Peyton entered his room and witnessed the baby escapee. When I entered the room and asked how in the world Camden got out of the bed, Peyton exclaimed with excitement, "I know, I'll show you." He climbed in Camden's bed and jumped off the side hit the floor, rolled, and faked cried. This moment is one of my favorite memories.

One of Peyton's favorite toys with his battery-powered John Deere gator. He spent many hours exploring our yard in his gator. Peyton also loved *Thomas the Train*. He knew all of the colors because of the trains and started to have a very big collection. Videos of Thomas were always playing in the background at our home.

Peyton also loved to swim. His nanny had a pool and he learned to swim by the age of three. He was a little fish. Peyton had the biggest,

In the Beginning

bluest eyes you had ever seen. And he always had a huge smile and a sparkle in his eyes (always filled with mischief). He lit up the room when he entered it. He never met a stranger. He was the easiest child to make laugh, and he laughed a lot! He was always dancing and moving. He could never keep still.

My life could not have been better. I had a wonderful marriage to my best friend, had two boys which I had always wanted and just moved into my dream home. Things in my life were going pretty perfect. Then, out of the blue, my oldest son dies. My world as I knew it disappeared in an instant.

Chapter 2

A Mom's Worst Nightmare

In October of 2006 we took a trip to Disney World. The weather was great; a perfect time to introduce the boys to Mickey Mouse at the "Mickey's Not-So-Scary Halloween Party." We were there a couple of days, and Peyton started to get sick. He started out with fever then vomiting. He would be okay a little while but then feel bad again. We were on our last day at Disney so decided to stay because the big trick-or-treat event was that night. He enjoyed himself for most of the day but just didn't have the energy we were used to him having. We left to come home the next day, and I took Peyton in to see the doctor. We were told he had a severe case of strep throat. The doctor said the vomiting with stomach cramps were all strep related. The pediatrician put him on antibiotics and sent us home.

As the day progressed, Peyton got worse. He couldn't keep anything down, including the medicine. We called my mother-in-law to come get Camden because we didn't want him to get sick. It took both me and Chad to take care of Peyton. I started to become very concerned after he continued to throw up to the point vomit came out of his mouth and he wouldn't move. We took him to the emergency room. After a thorough exam, the ER doctor came to the conclusion that he had strep and that all of his symptoms seemed to be because of the strep. They told us to give the antibiotic shot twenty-four hours to work before he should start to feel better. We returned home to much of the same. I stayed awake all night taking care of him, changing clothes, wiping him down, and checking his temp. I had to give him rectal Tylenol to keep his fever down.

The next day, he was horrible. After a sleepless night, I called Chad to come home from work to help me. We called the pediatrician's office and told of our ER visit and the exhausting night he had. We were told to give the antibiotic shot time to work then bring him in if there were no changes.

When Chad got home, I went to my bed for a quick nap. I had to return a phone call from my sister; as I lay in bed, I caught her up on all that was going on with Peyton. All of a sudden, I heard Chad yell with horror, "JENNIFER!!!" I came running in to find Chad yelling at Peyton to "BREATHE!" Chad had been holding Peyton in his arms on the couch when he felt Peyton gasp for his last breath of air. He ran to the car with Peyton in his arms saying, "We have to take him to the hospital!" He started the car while he was holding a lifeless Peyton. I was still on the phone with my sister and asked her what to do? She could hear everything in the background and told me to call 911. I got off the phone. Looking back, I see God used my sister to help us in our nightmare. Gena knew what was going on and began to call all of our family and get a prayer chain started.

With my world now stopped, I ran to get clothes and shoes on (Later, I would destroy those clothes because of the memories they held). Running to the car, I suddenly realized that if Peyton still wasn't breathing, he wouldn't make it to the hospital. I knew we had to do CPR and call an ambulance. Something stepped in giving me a clear mind. I grabbed Peyton out of Chad's arms and laid his limp body on the floor. I told Chad to call 911. When Chad got the 911 operator on the phone he handed it to me. "I know how to do CPR, but I've never actually done it please talk me through it." I exclaimed.

He asked me, "Is he choking?"

I cried, "No, he has been sick and isn't breathing."

The operator, again, asked, "Is there anything lodged in his throat?"

I screamed, "NO!!! He has not been able to eat!"

Again, "Are you sure he isn't choking?"

"Why are you continuing to ask me this? NO! Tell me how to do CPR!" I became very angry at the 911 operator. Looking back, I'm not sure if they are required to ask multiple times if someone is choking before CPR can be performed. But for me, it was very frustrating, and I felt each time he asked my child was losing hope of being revived. Finally, the operator talked me through the CPR. I did the unimaginable. For what seemed like eternity I did chest compressions and breathed for my child on our living room floor. Looking at him lying there lifeless, he seemed so tiny, so fragile. His eyes were open and non-responsive. I was worried about them drying out so I tried to close them but couldn't. Still Peyton didn't have a pulse nor was breathing on his own. Chad was pacing.

Finally, we heard the sirens of fire trucks. Chad ran outside to direct them. The medics came rushing in and I collapsed on the floor. I remember Chad grabbing me as the medics assisted Peyton. I kept saying, "He's gone, He's gone." The ambulance then arrived and as the medics entered, they started asking questions, quickly scooped him up and ran with him to the ambulance parked in our driveway. As I ran after them and stepped out of my garage, I remember thinking how bright it was and that this could not be happening. Our cul-de-sac was filled with fire trucks. The reality of it started hitting me, and I looked up and actually expected to see Jesus descending down from Heaven to save me from this nightmare. Old hymns and some of my favorite worship songs began playing automatically in my head: *Holy, holy, holy Lord God Almighty, Jesus, Jesus sweetest Name I know.* I didn't know why I heard them or where these songs were coming from. Over and over, they repeated in my head. I jumped into the ambulance and took the worst ride of my life. As we left, I saw Chad fall to his knees in the yard. I was praying, extending my hands to my son and praying loud for God to help!

The ride took an eternity. At one point the medic in the back called out, "we have his color back!"

A little hope entered my heart. I asked the driver, "How long can he live without oxygen to the brain?"

Knowing he hadn't been able to breathe on his own for a while. The driver said, "Well after six minutes there starts to be brain damage." I remember thinking, *God, I don't care if he has brain damage. I will take care of him for the rest of his life, just make him live!*

Upon arriving at the hospital, I was met by a group of people along with a chaplain. The chaplain took me to a little room where I had the chance to call my family. As she sat with me, I called my parents. They already knew a little about what was going on, so I gave them some more details. She told me they had made a bunch of phone calls and that everyone was praying for us, especially for the life of Peyton. As I got off the phone, the chaplain did her best to comfort me and told me that it was in God's hands. I knew that the doctors were doing all they could to help my son and that God was with them. It was out of my hands.

The driver of the ambulance walked into the room and had to ask me some procedural questions. I can close my eyes and still smell the cologne he was wearing. I looked into his eyes and felt his ache for me. I should have known something was severely wrong at that point. My aunt had been called so I was relieved when I saw her enter the room. Chad finally arrived at the hospital as did his parents a short time after. After a long period of time, the doctor and a nurse came in. They sat down and paused for a while. Then the doctor asked us what was going on with Peyton. I started to explain the events but paused and asked, "Is Peyton okay?"

The doctor held his head down, shook it and responded, "No, no he's not okay."

The next thing I heard was my mother-in-law screaming at the top of her lungs, "NO, NO, NO!!!"

I had to run out of the suffocating little room and into the hall. I couldn't handle the screams. I wanted to run, run as fast as I could out of that place. My world came to a screaming halt. All the staff around were staring at me. I couldn't breathe. I couldn't cry. I couldn't scream. Shock. Total shock took over. What all had just happened? Just a few days before I had a happy, healthy three-year-old running wild at Disney World. Everything was happening too fast. I had no time to prepare for it!

Now the doctors were asking if I wanted to see my son for the last time. It felt like I moved into another dimension. It felt as though the world actually stopped turning on its axis. I felt at any moment I was going to see God's face. God now had my baby. I just knew He was going to show me His face and explain what had just happened. Why He chose to take *my* little boy. At this moment, anything was possible. The most impossible thing I could have ever imagined just happened so anything else could be believable. Heaven became a reality. I knew it existed but had never given it a whole lot of thought. Now, I knew my precious boy was there. Heaven and earth began to become entwined. I now had a huge connection to Heaven. I could never have dreamed that, *There is no God*. How could anyone *ever* think that?

Everything was suddenly black and white—no shades of grey. I knew God was real. Heaven was real. The sudden death of a child—my child—was real. I was terrified. I didn't know what was next. The pain was so intense. Did the pain get worse? Could my body handle this pain? Fear gripped my whole being. What else could happen? My entire security was ripped out from beneath me.

Oh God, why? Why me? Why Peyton? What did I do? What did I not do? How could I go on? How could I leave this hospital with the body of my little boy still lying in the bed? My mind raced. *What next? What now?* My stomach churned. I felt so helpless. All I could tell myself was that God was in control and that He would take care of everything. I had to put it in His hands. What other choice did I have?

Chad and I were able to go say goodbye to Peyton. We walked down the hall into a room where our precious baby laid. He still had tubes coming out of his mouth. We were asked not to move him. I stroked his hair knowing it would be the last time I was going to be able to do it. He looked like he was sleeping. His eyes had been closed and he was just as beautiful as ever. I couldn't say goodbye, all I could say was that I would be with him really soon. We kissed him as we left the room. I had to make one of the worst decisions of my life, to leave my son behind at the hospital. We had to return home without him for the first time since his birth.

As we were leaving the hospital, the chaplain came up to me and put her forehead to mine. She asked me did I know where my little boy was at that moment. I said, "Yeah, I see him running into Jesus' arms!" She too saw the same vision. We both saw Peyton running down a beautiful path. I was just focused on his face. He had a huge smile as he was running. Jesus was kneeling down with his arms stretched out, and Peyton leaped into His arms. Jesus grabbed him and gave him a big hug. Peyton's laughter and hug with Jesus was a vision that would carry me for weeks. I saw my son's face as He saw Jesus' face for the first time. I believe God allowed me to see into Heaven to comfort me at those extremely difficult moments. He allowed the chaplain to see this vision as well for a confirmation so the Devil would not try to confuse me about what I just saw.

I didn't want to go back home. I never wanted to go back into that house ever again, especially right after Peyton's death had suddenly taken place. As we were exiting the hospital, my pastor was coming in. We embraced with little words to be said. He understood my grief as he had lost a twelve-year-old son. I told him my distress about going home. He explained that even though it would be difficult, it was the right thing to do.

The drive home was excruciating. Everything was in slow motion. We had to go pick up Camden from my sister-in-law. When we arrived, we had to take Peyton's car seat out. My sister-in-law was outside holding Camden. She looked at us with questions as she hadn't heard the news yet. Unable to speak, I shook my head and scooped Camden out of her arms.

Then, we went home. Friends and family had already heard the news. My house was already full of people. I spent the rest of the day throwing up and crying uncontrollably. I wanted my parents and sister there so bad. They were traveling from Jacksonville as fast as they could to get there. My parents had wonderful friends who volunteered to drive them because my parents couldn't drive in their condition.

Chad couldn't even come inside the house. He slept in his truck for a couple of days until he had the strength to stay inside. The next few days were a blur. I feel the Lord blocked me from so many emotions. It was though He gave me some sort of anesthesia. The pain was so intense but I knew the Lord was carrying me. I was experiencing a spiritual intervention. How else was I getting through each second? I felt then what it was like to be held, held by God and the prayers of all who loved me.

Shock

The day after Peyton died, we had to go up to the funeral home to make all of the arrangements. The Lord had been orchestrating the details ever since my birth. One of the things He did was allowing us to live next door to Mr. Woody McKown. He worked at the funeral home (no coincidence) and to our surprise, had lost his four-year-old daughter years before. He helped us with all of the arrangements and knew what we were going through. My sister and brother-in-law came with us for support that we desperately needed. We had to choose times, dates, pick out a casket and also where we wanted him buried. One of the hardest things to hear was that we were to pick out what clothes we wanted Peyton in and send them up to the funeral home.

As we were at the funeral home, the medical examiner called. She explained that Peyton was born with a congenital diaphragmatic hernia (CDH). He was born with a hole in his diaphragm and his stomach and spleen had herniated up into his chest cavity. His left lung was underdeveloped giving him little lung capacity. His heart had been shoved to the middle of his chest. They believed the strep put him over the edge.

As strange as it may sound, this revelation was actually a little bit of a relief to me and Chad. We then felt that we had no control over what had happened. In some strange way, death by strep throat made us feel more responsible for not acting appropriately. By having this birth defect, we got a little comfort at the time to think that he was a miracle for the time we had him.

The most difficult decisions of my life soon followed. Going back to our home, deciding what to put in the obituary, what to bury him in and with, what to say to his little brother, asking "Now what?"

Family, friends, flowers, hugs, tears, food, cards, phone calls, followed as well. The Lord blessed us with a huge support system. My family, as well as Chad's family, were there for us every minute in the days to follow. Our friends came from all over; high school friends we had lost touch with were here immediately. Our church family stepped in; food was coming from everywhere, as well as flowers. We had never felt so loved than in those days following Peyton's death. We could not have made it without them. Camden could not have made it without them. God knew who, how, and when we needed things. He placed everything and everyone in our lives just at the precise moment.

I don't remember too much about the wake. I do remember there was a huge outpouring of love from everywhere. We had at least 300 to 400 people show up to offer their condolences, a huge blessing in such a horrible time. My dearest friends, Amanda and Jennie, had taken it upon themselves to make a few beautiful displays with many pictures of Peyton.

I would have to say that the day of the funeral was the hardest, as were most of the first few days. I can't remember too many details. Bro. Dale Patterson gave Peyton a beautiful service. I have heard from a few people that they accepted the Lord as their Savior because of Bro. Dale's heartfelt words. Many would have never thought of doing so under any other circumstances. I was told that my precious father-in-law accepted Jesus that day too. The sudden death of a child has a way of opening people's eyes to the quickness life can be taken away.

When the funeral was over and everyone had left, we were sitting on our front porch when two stray dogs came running onto the porch. We lived in a neighborhood where seeing dogs running loose was rare. The two dogs ran up to us as if we were their family. One was a golden retriever mix and the other was a small shaggy shih tzu mix: an odd looking pair and two of the sweetest dogs I had ever met. The larger golden one, sat at my feet while the white one sat in my lap. As I loved on them talking to them, I forgot my sadness for a second. Neither had a collar, and they hung around with us until we went inside. I am an animal lover through and through. Looking back at our dog visit, I know it was no coincidence. God knows me better than anyone, and He knew I needed a visit from two shaggy angels which was the only thing at that moment that would comfort me.

Chapter 3

Starting a Life Without Peyton

Friday, Nov. 2006 – "Two weeks ago yesterday, I lost my precious little boy. Oh, how my heart aches. At times it doesn't seem real, believable. Then it hits so hard. Reality. I will never see Peyton again on earth. The pain is so unbearable. Then, I can feel the Lord holding me up. I am terrified, terrified of the next emotion. My heart is completely broken. The physical pain is so bad. I am empty, lonesome, lost, confused. Angry... I can't look at Peyton's pictures. It is too painful. And seeing his clothes and toys rips me apart, especially seeing his toothbrush. I miss him so much; his smile, his voice, his sparkly blue eyes. His I love yous, his giggles, his snuggling with me, his presence, and his joy. My world has stopped."

Days didn't exist now, just seconds and minutes. I could not possibly look toward tomorrow; I could only see one foot in front of the other, one breath at a time. That moment right then was so intense, so difficult. *How can I think about carrying this pain until tomorrow?* Nothing else existed for me either, just my family and God. No outside world, no television, no radio, no internet. Nothing else mattered, nothing else at all.

I was living my worst nightmare. I couldn't eat; the thought of me being able to enjoy food saddened me even more. I couldn't sleep. I lost weight. I would sit for hours in the dark listening to the Casting Crowns song *Praise You in This Storm* on repeat. I couldn't even leave my house for a long while. I didn't want to. Memories were everywhere. Most of the time, I would drive somewhere but didn't even have the strength to go inside.

My life now became "before Peyton" and "after Peyton." Places I had once been with Peyton were difficult—if not impossible—to go to. I chose to go to places and stores I had never been to before. The first time I went somewhere that Peyton had been with me, I broke down. Each of my memories were difficult. I started to wonder how parents that lost older children could cope with all of their years' of memories. Peyton had lived three years and eight months and each memory was difficult to visit. When I went to a store, I felt as though each person there should sense my pain and know what a loss I had suffered. Yet no one asked about him. Everyone was going on with their lives, laughing and acting as though life was great. Didn't they know what had just happened? My world was standing still, yet life around me was going on as though nothing had happened. I knew logically that strangers couldn't possibly know my son had died, but something deep inside me felt as though the whole world should be grieving for my son as well.

Anytime, anywhere someone would ask the question, because Camden was with me, "How many children do you have?" This question became a nightmare for me. *How should I answer?*

The first time I heard this question, I remember my heart crumble, "Two children."

"How old?" they would then ask.

"Camden is almost two and we just lost our son who was three and a half." The look of pity and shock filled the stranger's face. They became speechless, almost embarrassed that they had asked. It was as though I had just told them I had some kind of highly contagious disease.

People around me acted as though I had this "disease" that would jump on them if they got too close. Even family members would rather avoid me than approach me with the risk of me falling to pieces. *Didn't they know I was already in pieces?* Nothing they could say would cause them to "remind" me my son was gone. I thought about him each second. All I wanted and still want is to talk about him. For friends and family to show they care and miss him too. Others shared my pain but in a totally different way. Most could carry on—maybe not as if nothing had happened—, but when they went home, *their* home hadn't changed. A lot of friends and family avoided mentioning Peyton as if afraid I would fall apart if they did. Others I knew just gave me this look of such deep pity, afraid to approach me. Some just stopped talking to me altogether. There were even times friends and family caught me crying and for whatever reason chose to ignore me instead of trying to comfort me. My whole world had crashed, and I was not sure in the least bit how to handle it. I now viewed the world so different. The world viewed me so different—my world at least. My world had completely stopped in rotation. I felt so alone.

The only person that could possibly feel my pain was my husband; Chad became my rock. I looked at him with such different admiring eyes. I could visibly see he was a broken man, and the pain behind his eyes broke my heart every time I looked into them. Chad had never allowed his tears to flow easily. He never let his emotions take control over him. He felt he had to protect me, and he did. When I had to remind myself to breathe and felt I couldn't go on another second, he was there with amazing strength. God put the perfect comforting words into his heart to remind me of Who was in control. If it wasn't for Chad, I would have either died or been put into an institution.

I would start to be consumed with a deep fear. The rug had been pulled out from underneath me; my security was gone. I was in fear of my next emotion. *What could happen next?* I was afraid of hurting any *more* than I already did. The fear that I lived with was the fear of something happening to someone else around me—for death to suddenly snatch someone away from me again.

At the same time, I lost all my physical, earthly fear for myself. Personally, I felt I was untouchable—that no evil of this world could reach me. For example, I would go for walks in the middle of the night without the usual fear of someone stepping out of the shadows. Most of the time, it was as if I encouraged the Evil One to send someone my way to *try* to harm me. If I died, I would simply be with my son and escape this pain. My absolute worst fear had already come true. I was no longer afraid of what anyone thought of me. My voice for Jesus became loud and strong. I knew He was the only way to Heaven and I wanted to scream it from the rooftop. I wanted everyone I knew and loved—also those whom I did not know—to enter Heaven on the day of their death. There was no time to waste. I felt the urgency of it now.

Day after day, the truths and reality of what happened to my little boy just kept repeating itself. I couldn't sleep. My brain reeled and hurt from thoughts continually exploding in my head. I wanted to rest but couldn't. I was scared to fall asleep. When I awoke, it was like someone punched me right in the gut. The second my eyes opened, the pain was there waiting to invade my body again. I have heard that when you sleep your mind still believes your child is alive, so when you wake up, you relive that pain all over again. It takes a while for your subconscious to understand what a great loss you have just had. At times it did feel unreal—so unbelievable. My days crept by. *How can I go on with this pain for the REST of my life?* It was too much to deal with for just that day. I also started having these weird feelings like Peyton never existed. I guess it was hard to accept that he was gone, so my brain told me he was never here. I was having trouble accepting his death. I had trouble being around other children that were three years old. They gave me too many reminders of what I had lost.

Then a natural instinct soon overcame me, and I knew I had to face my new reality. I had to endure it. I had no other choice. There was no escape. My husband had just lost his precious little shadow, and he didn't deserve to lose a wife as well. The same went for Camden; he needed his mother now more than ever.

Why, God?

I had so many questions. How could this be? We were the happiest family around. We were close, loving, and together in everything. Couldn't we have been spared and found out about his deformities before now? Why didn't doctors see it? Could surgery have saved him? How could he have lived with no symptoms? Could I go through this and come out a decent person: wounded but not bitter, cautious but not paranoid, loving but not clingy? Why did God allow this to happen? Was I not on the right path? Did I just take too many things for granted? Who was I without Peyton? How can I be who I was? I was just the shell of Jennifer, now. It happens all over to so many different people. Why was it so hard to believe it could happen to *me*? What if I had never been able to have children? What if I had never married Chad? Could I have spared everyone this pain? Is this pain worth the sacrifice? Deep down I knew it was.

I would have Peyton and Camden all over again. He was such a special angel, such a gift. How can you cope with this devastation? Peyton held my heart. As his brother and daddy do still. *Is that why God took him—because I loved him too much? How do you not love your children more than God? They are my hearts running around outside my body. I just felt so lost—without a clue, scared. Could this happen again, death snatching something so valuable?* My child was gone. I cannot watch him grow, go to school, play sports, ride bikes, swim, play, graduate, nor get married. I will never meet his children. *When I see him in Heaven, what will that be like? How old will he be? Will we live together? Will I remember all of my anguish here on Earth? Will we talk about the same things? Will he still act and talk the same way? Still talk like a child? When will I go to Heaven? How can I live to be an old lady without my oldest son? Will Jesus come back before I am an old lady? What will I get in Heaven as a reward for my suffering? Just to be with Peyton again will be reward enough for me.* Even still, I was surer of things too. It was so confusing. Gone, I can't see him, hold him, can't hear his voice. It is hard to believe that many parents have to deal with this pain. Many parents have to deal with even more loss. Yet others never have to deal with this type of loss. I wanted him back so bad. But was that fair to him? Why did I have to live without him? How can I? I felt like after time went on, no one felt the way I did. Would I ever heal? Was I supposed to? Was I going to be okay?

I was consumed with grief and sadness. It killed me that in order to cope with life I had to leave Peyton's memory behind. I tried not to think of him, tried not to look at pictures. As if I were trying to forget him. I did not want to let go, ever. But how could I go on if I didn't? At times, the realization hit me out of nowhere and like a ton of bricks. Would I ever get to experience pure joy again? And if I did, would the guilt of feeling it steal it away? I was searching for answers, looking for my place in this world again. Where was I supposed to take these questions? I knew I would not ever be normal again.

Starting a Life Without Peyton

Who Am I?

My longing to see Peyton started to grow deeper. Each day that went by, the further and further away he became. The pain started touching deep down into my heart. I still couldn't think of him too much. If a thought about him came to mind, I had to think about something else. It hurt too badly. Even if I wanted to, I couldn't picture his face when I closed my eyes. I knew every square inch of his body, all of his expressions. So why couldn't I close my eyes and see his face? My memory was starting to become terrible. I wanted to think of things but I couldn't. I felt numb.

I became engulfed in this terrible sadness. I was empty. The pain in my stomach overpowered me. There was nothing I could do to escape this pain. The usual things that brought me joy no longer interested me. No where I could go would leave my pain behind. It followed me—even beat me to most places. Every single day was a struggle. I missed my son horribly. I wished I could just see his face, hear his laughter, hold him tight, and tousle his beautiful blonde hair. I began to wonder if I could come out of this pain. There was so much I could not understand. I wondered how God chose who to allow this to happen to.

I kept telling myself, *Just get through the day*. I became sick of hearing those words. I had been through the day, and yesterday, and the day before that. The pain just kept coming. I couldn't see the light at the end of the tunnel. I felt I was in a deep pit looking up and barely seeing light with everyone just looking down at me. I began to withdraw. It was very difficult to engage in simple conversation again. Listening to others complaining made me resentful.

I started having trouble talking to Chad. When I cried to him, it made him upset. Most members of my family were the same way.

I had trouble expressing myself because I was unfamiliar with all of these new, dreadful emotions. I was scared to share my real feelings with others. I was scared, too, of these feelings I was having. If I said it out loud, my reality seemed worse. If I spoke about it to others, they cried. I didn't want to make anyone cry anymore. I lost friends. Some family distanced themselves from me. It was hard to find someone who understood what I was going through. I tried going to a support group but it was difficult watching so many people in such pain. I felt isolated and alone. It was hard to get back to the real world.

A New Life

In my home, I was learning how to be a mom of one child again. My house seemed too quiet and empty. The sounds in my home changed dramatically: no more running, screaming, laughing children. Everything around our home had changed. Everywhere I looked were reminders that Peyton was just recently with us. His toys, his handprints on the window and wall, his train tracks stuck in random places, his dirty clothes, his pictures on the refrigerator, and his toothbrush were agonizing reminiscent of my son.

Camden was lost. He didn't know how to play by himself. He had never had to; Peyton (Tay Tay to Camden) had always been his source of entertainment. I started grieving for Camden and his loss. Camden became *my* shadow. He had taken on a role far exceeding his time. He started trying to nurture me. He also started gaining a new character trait; trying to make me smile. He learned very quickly of certain things he could do or say to bring a smile to my face. But it was difficult to make me laugh.

My front porch became my sanctuary. I spent many hours and countless tears there. I was there all hours of the night because I couldn't sleep. My relationship with Jesus began to deepen there. It is where I really got to know who God really is. He was the only one I could be my real self with, the only one I could share my deepest anguish with. He felt more real than ever. He became my friend, not just a character of the Bible. Not just my God that I say the blessings and bedtime prayers to or worship on Sunday mornings. He became a part of me. I started seeing through a filter. Truths screamed out at me. The world with all of its problems became clear as black and white. I had begun a big change.

Camden was also changing; he began seeing into the walls of heaven. God had blessed him with an amazing gift. With his innocence, our openness and gaping wounds, God was giving us miracles. We didn't realize how miraculous this gift would become nor how it would help in our healing process unlike anything else in this world could.

Chapter 4

God Steps In

Blessed are those who mourn, for they shall be comforted.
                    Matthew 5:4 (KJV)

Just days before, I knew what my son was doing every second of each day. I fed him, played with him, brushed his teeth, bathed him, he slept with us. Now, I had no idea what he was doing all day. I felt so lost without him. All of our routines, my routines, were gone, just like he was. I pleaded with God to let me know what Peyton was doing.

One morning shortly after Peyton's death, I was lying in the bed crying. All the sudden, I saw Peyton. He had a huge smile on his face. As I looked closer, I saw that he was being carried by an angel. The angel had his arms under Peyton's armpits and was flying him around. The angel would skim the ground with Peyton's dangling feet and then fly upwards. The angel never flapped his enormous wings. He was just "coasting" through heaven. All the sudden, they came to a huge body of beautiful clear water and the angel let Peyton go. Pey Pey went under. I remember thinking in my earthly mind, *Oh no, Peyton can't swim!* But Peyton popped out of the water with an enormous grin, completely dry! I saw how much fun my little boy was having in his new home. It was just a glimpse God had given me that to this day is so vivid in my mind.

Heaven started to overwhelm my daily thoughts. I started reading all the books I could get my hands on from Christian authors about heaven. I started imagining what Peyton was doing in Heaven.

I wondered who was taking care of him or if he even needed to be looked after. I was now excited and eager to go there. But I knew it wasn't my time yet. I vowed to make the most of my time now here on earth. I vowed to try to live with nothing left unsaid nor undone.

My pastor had begun to counsel with me, an amazing man who had lost his twelve-year-old son years before. As I was en route to one of my appointments, I noticed a big cloud that looked like an angel. She had a trumpet in her hands and a long train behind her. The cloud was being blown by the wind and I told myself "That was neat! That sure looked like and angel!" Believing I had imagined the angel in the clouds.

During my talk with my pastor, we discussed angels. He said that there was this one time he was doing a funeral and as he was facing the setting sun, he noticed a cloud that was perfectly shaped like an angel. He described her blowing a trumpet and that she had a long train. I began to sob. He had described exactly what I had just seen (although the cloud angel I had seen wasn't as perfectly formed). God had not wanted me to pass it off as my imagination. He had given me the same gift from heaven as He had given my pastor.

In the throes of my grief, I began to beg the Lord to show me angels. I knew they were all around me; I could feel them now more than ever. I just wanted to see into the spirit world. That would bring me some comfort. "Please Lord; allow me to see my angels!"

As I laid there, the Lord put my eyes on a large picture of Camden. Then the Lord spoke to my spirit and said, "I am not going to give you a *glimpse* of an 'angel,'(I never thought God meant an actual angel) for I have given one to be with you twenty-four hours a day to bring you comfort." These words were powerful, an instant wake up call. I knew then what I had to do. I was about to start learning exactly what the Lord meant when He said Camden was my "angel."

God Steps In

We miraculously got through the holidays that followed Peyton's death. It was no easy task. Peyton's birthday was approaching, as was Camden's second birthday. Camden's birthday is 5 days before Peyton's. I have come to realize the anticipation of Peyton's birthday is worse than his actual birthday. We made it through and I now understood what it is meant to be "covered in prayer." We had a protection, a guard around us that whole day. God is amazing.

I had spoken with the medical examiner and found out the details about Peyton's death. Before she explained all of her findings, she told me how beautiful my son was. She saw signs that he was loved very much. She went on to tell me how she loved his hair and she could tell how well we took care of him because his toenails and fingernails were neatly groomed. That was hard to hear but it also let me know that the medical examiner saw Peyton, not just a body in which to determine the cause of death. She really took him in, which meant a lot to me. She explained in detail about the hole in his diaphragm and his hernia. She said he was born with the hernia because his stomach was in the middle of his chest cavity. She also said he had very little left lung capacity because the heart grew into that space. Questioning her, I asked "How could he have been born this way without symptoms?" She kept reiterating that she only goes by what she finds and that she was positive he was born with this diagrammatic hernia. Other doctors who viewed this would also question it. I talked to the medical examiner three times questioning her and she kept telling me she didn't care what other doctors said about her report, that she stands behind her findings and she had been in this profession for decades.

I got the death certificate on a Tuesday. The Lord spoke to me telling me that I would be receiving a package the day the death certificate came. I began to dread when the mail ran. One day when

I came home, my heart sank. I noticed the mail had just run. I inched towards the mail box. But the Lord spoke and said, "It isn't here because your package isn't here." As He said, there wasn't any certificate.

A few days later, driving in the driveway I noticed a big box on my front porch. "This is it, huh, Father. If I heard you right it's here today." I grabbed my package and went to the mailbox. Sure enough, the dreaded envelope was in there. As God had promised, He had sent me backup to help cushion the pain. I went to the front porch not so sure what to open first. I chose the death certificate. What a dreadful piece of paper, confirming my son's death. I had received two birth certificates in the mail that looked pretty similar to this except for the word DEATH screaming at me. I sobbed at the reality of the paper laying it aside. *Now Lord, my gift from you;* I opened the box and read the note inside, "Your sister picked out this purse for you a while back. I am just now getting it to you, sorry for the delay." I opened the gift: a beautiful purse with the embroidered words, "I can do all things through Christ who strengtheneth me" (Philippians 4:13 (KJV)).

Wow! I can do this through Christ, not through myself. I called my sister, thanked her, and told her about what God had said about the package. She hung up with me and called Aunt Laura describing what I had shared. Aunt Laura had told her that she had had the purse a little while but hadn't had a chance to send it. Then one day out of the blue, her young daughter told her that they needed to mail the package that day. She said it was a rainy, ugly day, and she hadn't any errands to run so hated to get out in the weather. But her daughter insisted that they send it THAT day! Isn't God amazing? He has perfect timing.

The night I received the package and death certificate we got a visit from a couple in our church that also lost a child. They comforted us and the woman told me she had a scripture for me: "I can do all things through Christ who strengthens me!" God wanted to make *sure* I knew that I could do this with Him by my side!

Chapter 5

Camden's Gifts

March 22, Tuesday. A couple of days ago we were riding in the car and Camden said, I want to go to Pey Pey's house. I said, you do? And he said, "Yeah, Pey Pey's house is in the sky. I said "That's right. Pey Pey's house is in the sky in Heaven". He said, "There's a gate; a big gate. A big pretty gate. And water; pretty water and fireworks, pkew, pkew (the sound fireworks would make)! Fireworks and pretty water."

And the twelve gates were twelve pearls, every several gate was of one pearl.
Revelation 21:21 (KJV)
And he shewed me a pure river of water of life clear as crystal, proceeding out of the throne of God and of the Lamb.
Revelation 22:1 (KJV)

We have never spoken of Peyton having a house in heaven nor of the gates or the water. And fireworks? I wish I could see what he saw. How amazing for my child, who just turned two, tell me these things—what a blessing from God. He knows where his brother is. We don't even have to tell him.

Camden was 20 months old when Peyton passed away. He wasn't speaking very much: a few words and fewer broken sentences. After his big brother passed away, he started speaking and using wonderful English. He had known how to use lots of words; he just didn't need to until now. He kept asking where "Pey Pey" was. We would tell him that God needed "Pey Pey" in Heaven. Camden had never played by himself. He didn't know how. He could see the pain in everyone's face around him, and he became our little comforter. I was afraid my horrible crying outbursts were going to cause him tremendous emotional damage. But as I counseled with my pastor, he assured me that it was good for Camden to see me cry. That it would show him how much we loved and missed his brother. That crying was a good emotion. Just not to allow myself to cry continuously and not be there for my youngest son. Each time I cried, Camey asked what was wrong. I continually told him that I was missing "Pey Pey." He would bring me tissues and rub my back. He soon began to say, "Miss Tay Tay?" (he couldn't say "Pey Pey"), when I would start to cry.

Chad and the boys had a thing between them that whenever Chad would talk to them on the phone or when he was looking for them, he would yell "Ka-Kaw, Ka-Kaw!" (from a movie we had seen) Peyton had really gotten into this little game with his daddy. He would always answer back and had even begun the game on his own by calling his daddy. Camden loved the game as well but hadn't caught on to it as his big brother had. A few weeks after Peyton's death, we were in the car and all of a sudden Camden said with such excitement, "Ka-Kaw, Tay-Tay, Ka-Kaw!" I asked him if he saw Peyton and with a huge eyes, big smile he nodded and looked into the sky. I wanted to flood him with questions, but he was too little at this time to answer them. I knew by his reaction and his body language that he did indeed see and hear his brother.

Camden started *knowing* his brother was in Heaven. He stopped asking where his big brother was. He went from asking all the time where Pey Pey was to stopping all together. God was allowing him to *see* where his brother was.

Another day, while riding in the car Camey looked out of the window and said with excitement holding his hands out, "Kank-ewe Tay-Tay!" His whole demeanor changed. He lit up and had a huge smile on his face. Then about 2 weeks after, Cam and I were snuggling in bed. He looked up at the window and said, "Tay-Tay!"

I asked if he saw Peyton, and he nodded. When I asked where, he pointed to where he was first looking. I wondered if Peyton could see us or if God just gave Camey a look into Heaven to see what Peyton was doing. It comforted Camden since he didn't understand where his brother was. It also comforted me by watching his whole disposition change to excitement. I KNOW he saw Peyton by the way he lit up and how happy he sounded. A two-year-old can't come up with such excitement and expression like that without seeing something.

Peyton has a baby!

Saturday, Nov. 2006 - My dear sweet Peyton, Oh, how much I love you. I miss you so very much. This all happened too quickly. You were so well then got so sick. I am so sorry that we didn't know what was going on with your body. But I know that Jesus didn't want us to find out. I want you to know how much you changed my love. You made my life so wonderful. You brought me more happiness that I never knew existed. The joy you gave me is beyond words. Thank you for giving me so much love and affection. You always gave me so many kisses and I love yous. I will never forget anything about you and your life.

About a year after Peyton died, I found out I was pregnant again. I was filled with mixed emotions. I was scared. Could I possibly be ready for this? Still deeply grieving, I thought that this might help by bringing something positive into our lives. Chad and I had become very close. Being intimate was not for pleasure at this time but to feel the oneness and closeness to each other. I was concerned that others would believe I wanted to become pregnant to replace Peyton. I could never replace my beloved firstborn.

Almost a month after I found out I was pregnant, my doctor gave me some horrible news. The ultrasound showed that I had what the professional world calls a "blighted ovum." A blighted ovum (also known as "anembryonic gestation") happens when a fertilized egg attaches itself to the uterine wall, but the embryo does not develop. A high level of chromosome abnormalities usually causes a woman's body to naturally miscarry. The placenta can continue to grow and support itself without a baby for a short time, and pregnancy hormones can continue to rise, which would lead a woman to believe she is still pregnant. A diagnosis is usually not made until an ultrasound test shows either an empty womb or an empty birth sac. The doctor wasn't sure how long this false pregnancy would last. I had to wait until my body passed the embryo. I thought I was okay with this. I kept telling myself that this wasn't meant to be. It comforted me some to know that there wasn't an actual life growing inside me.

Then, the news hit me. It was another hard blow. I was beginning to be happy about this pregnancy because it gave me something to look forward to. Now I was back to my usual pain. I now had more pain to deal with. I wasn't sure I had enough strength left in me. I became scared to leave the house. What if I was in public and I started to miscarry? All I wanted to do was to seclude myself even more at home.

Camden's Gifts

A couple of weeks later, I went in for my doctor's appointment to discuss a D&C; dilation and curettage. I was so confused. *If God allowed me to get pregnant, should I step in and do this?* The doctor assured me that there wasn't a baby, so this would not be like terminating a pregnancy. I had become a prisoner in my home, so with this procedure, I could finally leave the house. Also, each day that I was pregnant was a horrible reminder that I wasn't going to have a baby; just a day to day wait, which put me in a place where I couldn't move forward. I needed closure. I reluctantly agreed to have a D&C. I insisted on having another ultrasound before the procedure to make sure there wasn't a baby. I prayed and prayed over this the next few days asking God to make me comfortable with this decision if this is indeed what He wanted me to do.

I wasn't doing too well at home. One afternoon, I was laying in bed with Camden while he was napping. As he slept I watched him, trying to absorb all that was happening. I was in deep prayer begging for comfort.

The second Camden's eyes opened he gave me a huge hug and said, "Pey Pey likes to do dat!" He smiled, gave me another humongous hug and said it again, "Pey Pey likes to do dat!"

The day came when I had to go in for my procedure. As I lie there on the table looking at the monitor, the nurse and I saw the same thing, a baby. There wasn't any heartbeat but in fact a baby did form. The results from my blood work revealed that all of my levels were not the normal levels they were supposed to be for a healthy pregnancy. The baby was also underdeveloped and smaller than it was supposed to be at this point. Once I saw the form of my baby, there was no way I was going to go through with the procedure. The embryo had developed. I went home with more questions than answers but also relief that God had made it clear to me what I should do. I had a glimmer of hope that maybe just maybe they could also be wrong about the heartbeat. If I could go from definitely having a "blighted ovum" to having a baby form without my body absorbing it then there was a chance that God could allow the baby to be healthy and form normally.

As the high levels of chromosomes and ultrasound predicted, I miscarried at 12 weeks. When I say I reached an ultimate low, it is an understatement. I was crushed. The saddest part for me was that I felt God had let me down. *How could He have allowed this to happen so soon after Peyton's death? Once again could he have sparred me from this pain? If He knew I was going to miscarry, why did He allow me to see a baby inside of me?* Having to deal with just a false pregnancy was one thing but now I was grieving an unborn child.

Being so young, Camden had no idea of these events. Early in the pregnancy we had told him I was pregnant. But later when he asked about the baby in my tummy, I just told him that there wasn't a baby. At his age, he was fine with that answer. We didn't feel any need for further explanation.

A few days after my miscarriage, Camden and I were riding in the car. From the back seat I heard his little voice exclaim, "Peyton has a baby!" At first this comment didn't register.

Then it hit me what he had just told me. I swerved off the road—to this day, I still remember the exact spot—, put the car in park, turned around looking him in the eye, and asked, "What did you just say?"

This time with hand gestures he said excitedly, "Peyton has a BABY, Mama!"

Stunned, I asked, "Is Peyton holding the baby?"

"No" he said shaking his head. "Jesus is!"

The tears flowed. I was overjoyed. God had told my little boy where my baby was. He was safe in the arms of Jesus. This comforted me more than words. Now Peyton had a piece of our family with him in Heaven, a brother or a sister!

The next day Camden ran up to me and asked out of the blue, "What is that baby's name mama?"

Having a friend who just had a baby and NOT expecting the next words that came out of his mouth, I asked, "What baby?"

He said matter-of-factly in his baby voice, "Er baby. Er baby in heaven with Jesus. What is er baby's name?"

Once again I began to sob. Not only had he known that Peyton had a baby in Heaven, he also knew that the baby was MY baby. At this point, I relieved all my grief for this unborn child. I celebrated the fact that now I had two children awaiting me in heaven.

God Talks

A couple of months before Camden turned three, he asked if I had ever met God. I told him that I hadn't. He responded by saying, "I have. And He is so proud of you, Mama!"

Camden began talking about God A LOT! He asked a bunch of questions about Him. When we went to a water park, he'd ask many questions. Who made God? How big is God? Where does He live in heaven? Did He have a car? And my favorite, did God wear shoes? He then began asking a question, then pausing to answer his own question as if he was receiving the answer. He once asked if God had a pool. Then right after said, "Yeah, He does have a pool; a really big pool. It has water that is very pretty, you can see all the way to the bottom. There are tons of fish—big ones in it that won't even bite!"

He told me that God was *big*. He was amazed at how big God was. He also told me that God was silly. He told me that God sits in a really big chair. I asked Him if He knew what the chair was called but he didn't. I told him it was God's throne. I told him that angels circled His throne.

He said, "Really? I didn't see them!" He was two and a half at this time.

One day, when Camden and I were talking, he told me that Peyton was doing "boingeys" in heaven. Peyton and my sister had a game they played when my sister would come into town. He would always run from her. In order to get him to come to her, she would ask if he wanted to do boingeys. He would sprint toward her; she would hold him in her arms and bounce him really high. This was a special game between Peyton and his Aunt Gena. Because it had been a while since Camden heard the word or if he would have remembered it, I asked if he knew what boingeys were. He exclaimed, "Yes. It is when you jump high and higher to the lights!"

Speechless, I let it sink in. Then I asked him, "Does Peyton talk to you?"

He nodded his head. So, I asked, "What does he talk to you about?"

"He talks about God to me," was his amazing response. This answer made so much sense. That Peyton talked about God to Camden. Camden had spoken so much about God the past few weeks; He had been a constant topic in our daily conversations.

Excited about what he had just shared with me, I immediately called Gena. I told her what Camden had just told me about Peyton doing boingeys in heaven. That he could also describe what boingeys were. My sister on the other end of the phone was silent. Then I began to hear her sob. She said that just a few minutes before my call she was in bed crying missing Peyton. She prayed and wondered what Peyton was doing in heaven, and God used Camden to give her an answer at the perfect time!

Camden's Gifts

God Made Peyton Giggle

Camden came up to me one day and said laughing, "God made Peyton giggle. Really, really, really giggle."

He didn't know how God made him giggle just that he was laughing. As he was telling me about this vision, he began to belly laugh. Later that day I received a phone call from my mother. She began to tell me that her friend Roger had just explained to her a vivid vision he had of Peyton. Roger explained that He saw Jesus sitting on a large rock overlooking a garden. He saw that Jesus had a huge smile on his face. All he could hear was giggles, lots and lots of bubbly giggles around Jesus. He couldn't see anyone but Jesus, but he understood that the giggles were from Peyton. Roger felt like Jesus was telling him that He was so happy to have Peyton. He called my mom just after his vision and confirmed what Camden had shared with me earlier.

Chapter 6

A New Family

Savannah Peyton

Sometime in September of 2007 I found out I was pregnant. Again, I was filled with mixed emotions: excited, nervous, scared. Because of my past miscarriage, Chad and I chose not to tell anyone, not even Camden. We planned to wait until my second trimester to share the news.

I was in the kitchen, and Camden ran up to me pretending he was shooting me. He said, "Wait, I need to shoot that baby in your tummy!" Camden was a very active, imaginative hunter so while this took me a little by surprise, I couldn't imagine he could have known about the baby.

A little later that night, just to be sure, I asked Chad if he had told Camden anything about me being pregnant. As I suspected, he had not. I thought nothing more of it.

A week or so after the incident, I was lying on the couch when Camden ran up to me and kissed my tummy then ran back to playing. Kisses were not unusual for Camden because he was a very loving little boy. Then again, he ran up to me and kissed my tummy. I was only a few weeks along, so I had not begun to show. Laughing I asked him, "What are you doing?"

He said, "I'm kissing that baby in there." Shocked I looked at Chad to make sure he heard. Chad's mouth dropped, and he just shook his head. I began to cry, not only because Camden knew about the baby, but because I felt that God was revealing to me that my baby was going to be fine.

Being pregnant for any mom is a rollercoaster of emotions. For me it was a rollercoaster on steroids! I was excited about this wonderful life in my tummy, but I was also worried. *Would I be able to bond with this child after losing Peyton?* I was scared to have an unconditional love for this child and make me to be vulnerable to pain again.

Our Savannah Peyton (named after her big brother Peyton) came into the world on May 7, 2008 (Peyton was born on the 7th of the February). Our new miracle had been born in the delivery room before the doctor could arrive. She traveled through the birth canal so fast that her color was blue. After a few scary minutes and an exam from the NICU doctor, we let out a sigh of relief for she was perfect. For our peace of mind, Savannah's pediatrician had her x-rayed to make sure all her organs were where they were supposed to be which they were.

Our color at home now changed from blue to lots of pink. Camden instantly bonded with his little sister. She was given to us at the perfect time; she was just what we needed in our family to help us heal.

Hug from Heaven

The birth of Savannah made me really miss her big brother. Peyton was missed especially when we came home from the hospital as a "new" family. I ached for him to be a part of this. I wondered if he knew about his new sister. *Was he able to look down and see her?* This desire brought up a bunch of new emotions. I asked the Lord to help me cope with this new pain. I asked if He could show me that Peyton was a part of all of this.

A few days after I came home from the hospital, I woke up to what felt like someone giving me a big hug. The electricity went through my body, and although my eyes were closed, I saw a bright light. I thought, *Wow, Jesus was that you?* Then I thought I was probably imagining it because I was so tired. I fell back to sleep. I woke up again to the same experience. I still passed it off as that I was delusional from exhaustion.

All the next day I could not quit thinking about it. I could still feel the squeeze of the hug. The day after, Camden came up to me, hugged me, looked me in the eyes and said, "Peyton is supposed to give you a hug from Heaven!" He also told me that Peyton said for "you to live your life."

Speechless, I knew my experience wasn't all in my head but straight from heaven. God had answered my prayers once again. I was thrilled to know that Peyton had indeed been right there with us.

Having Savannah showed me the impact Peyton's death had on Camden. I would hear him tell Savannah, "I love you, so please don't die." He checked her regularly to make sure she was okay. In the weeks after birth, my mother stayed in our home helping with Savannah. One night when my mother had Savannah, Camden began to panic when he checked on her and couldn't find his sister. He ran into my room asking where she was and I calmed him by telling him Savannah was in Nana's room.

I Can Feel God's Presence

In my grief I started becoming someone new. I was seeking God like never before, and I found Him. My pain was still there, but I could see how a little light was coming through. I started noticing God's creation with appreciation. The things that God has made seemed more beautiful. Creation began to feel like it was created just for me. When the birds sang, I appreciated their song. When it rained, I enjoyed each drop like I had never experienced true rain before. I started noticing bugs; I started watching bugs with all of their detail. God put so much into giving the tiniest creatures beauty. If He cared so much about these tiny bugs, how much more did He care about me! Trees seemed more massive and stronger. The wind felt as if God was blowing in my face. The sun was like God opened a crack from heaven and His glory was shining through. I would lay in my front yard and absorb it into me (I know my neighbors thought I had lost it!). Colors seemed more brilliant. The stars, oh how stargazing made me feel closer to Heaven; they seemed magical.

Laughter was now an intoxicating sound and personal. In those early months, true laughter was a gift from God himself.

The love I had for my family didn't increase, but I became more aware of what it means to really love someone and to have them love me back. Love became such a precious gift. To hear Camden's voice brought me the best joy my life had to offer. Hearing him laugh, sing, tell me he loves me started to mend my heart a little piece at a time. Looking at my precious new baby girl, I knew I was beginning to heal. I treasured each second with my family, with everyone. Things that were once taken for granted every day were now so appreciated each second. I thought very little about the things that once were so important, the things that took up so much of my time.

First thing in the morning of my birthday, July 17 of 2008, I received a phone call from my sister Gena. She began to tell me of the awesome experience she had just had and explained that she had a difficult morning getting my niece and nephew off to school. She came back to the house and decided to go back to bed because she was feeling really sad. As she laid there, she suddenly saw Peyton. She said he was lying beside her. She just stared at him and thought, *No, this can't be Peyton.* She asked aloud, "Peyton?"

He turned, looked at her and said, "Yeah?"

She said his hands were folded behind his head like he always used to do. She was thinking, *How could this be Peyton? What should I say? I don't want him to leave.* She said, "I love you Peyton."

He looked back at her and said in his baby voice, "I wub you, too."

She told him how much she missed him. She said he looked at her with a very strange and confused look as if he didn't understand what she was talking about. She said she held his hand. She then asked him, "Do you miss your mama? You live with Jesus now. Are you happy with Jesus?"

She said that at this comment, Peyton's face lit up. She said he began to glow, became transparent, then disappeared. Gena felt that Peyton was trying to let us know how happy he is in Heaven, that to him, it is as if we are still a part of his life. She said she could remember every little detail about him, even how he felt. She said he had the look of pure joy on his face and radiated with happiness. She couldn't wait to tell me of her experience; then, she remembered it was my birthday! She began telling me how real it was. She said, "I even know what he was wearing."

I asked her to describe it.

She said, "Well, it was mismatched pajamas. The shorts were blue with something red on them and his shirt was white."

I began to cry because she had described the clothes he had on when he passed away. She had never known what he was wearing. God allowed Gena to see this detail to validate her vision.

God Orchestrates Details

One of my favorite spots to think was in our boat parked in the driveway and my favorite time to think was at night. I would put on music, lay down, and watch the stars. One particular night, I was talking to God. I would ask Him a question, and God would answer me with music. This conversation continued for a while. It is really difficult to explain how this affected me. I began to know God in a way I never thought possible. He had orchestrated each song at the perfect time to allow my questions to be answered. This encounter with God was the most intimate experience I had or have had since. He revealed more to me in that experience than I could have ever dreamed of. Couldn't the same God who spoke the universe into existence speak to my heart with music allowing me to feel closer to Him in my desperate time of need?

While I was in this closeness with God, I asked Him a very difficult question, with respectful reverence. I understood that God knew my pain, for He took our pain upon Himself in the flesh as Jesus on the cross. But I didn't understand how He could know how it felt to lose a child—as a mother who gave birth to her child after carrying him for nine months. His response was amazing. He spoke to my spirit revealing to me that His love is different from my love. He loves each of his children with more love than I could possibly imagine. More love than an earthly mother could ever have for her son. Not only does He have One Child, but He has many for whom He grieves with a grief I couldn't comprehend. He grieves for each and every one of His children that reject Him. As God revealed this to me, I began to weep, fully understanding what He meant. I apologized and felt a guilt because I questioned God, but I knew I had to ask hard questions to understand who He was.

One morning I was taking Camden to get his haircut. As Camden sat in the chair, I noticed a man looking at Camden and studying him. The man mentioned how handsome Camden was, which struck up a conversation. He said he had a grandson about Camden's age.

A New Family

The man told me the reason he was getting his haircut was because he was traveling to go to his grandson's funeral. There in the salon, God had orchestrated a tender moment. He told me that his grandson was accidentally shot when a gun fell from the gun cabinet and went off. I was very emotional and began to share my story. I asked him if it was okay if I got his daughter's address from him to send her some things that helped me through my grief.

His eyes lit up, and he said, "You can call her."

I told him that I wasn't sure she was ready to talk to a stranger, but I would start by mailing her a package. We walked out of the salon together. He told me how much our run-in helped him. We exchanged some comforting words, hugged, and left to go about our day. Nothing happens by chance.

She and I corresponded for a while. It is still amazing to me how much God loves us; He loves this grieving mom so much that He arranged for her father and I meet so God could encourage her.

Another morning, I was looking out the window into my front yard. I saw a cardinal sitting in a tree close by. I said to God, "He's beautiful but I'm not sure if You put him there for me."

God spoke to my spirit and said, "Well, how about a squirrel?"

Just then a squirrel ran up the same tree as the cardinal without the cardinal moving. I giggled wondering if this was just all in my head.

Then God spoke again, "How about a cat?" At that moment a cat ran right in front of the tree.

Laughing I asked, "Okay, how about a dog?"

At this, my dog Binkey began barking! As I am writing this, it seems hard to believe this could happen. But as Scripture says, God is close to the brokenhearted and crushed in spirit. This was how my God was comforting me.

Early one October morning, I awoke suddenly feeling God speaking to me. "Go outside, I have something to show you!"

Looking at the clock, which said 3:00 a.m. (This began what I call my "God time." He often woke me up at this time to reveal things to me.), I went outside to find a very brisk, clear night. I wrapped my blanket around me as I laid down to watch the beautiful night sky. Suddenly, I saw a shooting star, then another, and another. It was a glorious display of God's creation. I saw a total of six shooting stars within thirty minutes. I told the Lord "Thank you, they were beautiful."

He spoke to my heart and said, "So are you."

A few nights after this I was at my bible study I shared this experience with my group. One of the ladies spoke up and said that it could have been a meteor shower. When I got home, I looked it up on the computer and sure enough, there was a meteor shower that night! The article said that the best time to see it was 3:00 am, the time God woke me.

Bristol Nichole

I had just returned home from visiting my parents. Chad and I had a discussion and come to an agreement that we both felt we were not wanting any more children. I had thought on this subject many times but especially as I traveled. I told Chad I was happy and content with our four children, and he told me he had been feeling the same way. We decided to make a doctor's appointment to discuss a way to prevent future pregnancies.

Upon returning from the appointment, I began feeling really sick. I had a hard time sleeping. I was also more emotional than normal. Not being able to shake this feeling from my mind, I thought

A New Family

that maybe, just maybe I was pregnant. I went to get a pregnancy test just to be sure. Only a short time later the little strip turned positive! God was not ready for us to stop rearing children because my family wasn't complete yet.

Anxious because Savannah was only twelve months at the time, we shared the news with our family. All were excited. We didn't care if our baby was a boy or a girl as long as the baby was healthy. Soon, we found out that we could pass down all the pink: Savannah and Camden were getting a new little sister. I began to understand that Savannah and Bristol would be close just like Peyton and Camden were. As Camden grew, I longed to see Peyton grow with him, to watch that brotherly bond grow. God restored the sibling bond that I couldn't have with my boys by allowing me to watch my two little girls have this bond—a bond I that prayed would be as tight as my relationship is with my own sister.

On January 6, 2010, Bristol Nichole entered the world! She was our super surprise from God, and she was a joyful blessing. She entered this world as if she had always been meant for our family. She was a perfect fit.

There were only twenty months between Savannah and Bristol, which showed that God wanted to keep me busy! Thinking about the age differences of my children, I realized that Bristol was born seven years after Peyton. In Scripture, the number seven means completion. God revealed to me what He had told me years before, "Your family isn't complete yet." He had spoken these words to my heart a week after Peyton died because I was begging Him to allow an accident to take my life and allowing me to be with Peyton without me having to cause harm to myself. Bristol, born seven years after Peyton making our family complete, finished what God had promised five years before.

Chapter 7

Trapped in Grief

Even with the birth of my girls, I was only happy at surface level, but I tried to make myself believe that I was happy. Through months of counseling, I realize that I lived in my grief and could not define who I was without it. I was constantly looking in the rear view mirror waiting for something else to happen. I never truly let go of either my pain or my fear. I wasn't allowing God to reach deep down in my heart to wipe away those tears. I felt I needed those tears to keep Peyton a part of my life, that it would do him a dishonor if I let God wipe away *all* my tears.

I would have panic and anxiety attacks regularly and was diagnosed with Post Traumatic Stress Disorder. A certain pitch in someone's voice that to me indicated trouble, would sent me into a tailspin. A bunch of things became triggers for my attacks: sirens, screaming, hearing my name yelled, etc. I began to have such horrible anxiety that I would physically tremble when my PTSD was triggered, have a massive breakdown with tears, and would shut down once the anxiety dissipated. I had to be put on medication to control this cycle.

I had strings—debilitating anxiety, irrational fears, PTSD, and tremendous grief—attached to me from October 19, 2006, strings that wouldn't let me go. I became scared to cut those strings. This anxiety would begin to cripple me, allowing me to put up walls of protection which I used to isolate myself from the world in order to protect myself.

I started making many different excuses for myself, allowing me to stay in a dark place. But these walls I built were also keeping me from experiencing true happiness again. I was protecting myself so much that I began to lose sight of who God had made me to be. I was losing sight of the desires of my heart. I wasn't able to look forward to my future. I couldn't imagine what my future was going to be like. It was not until years later that I began to imagine my future and have hopes for it. I was so focused on getting through the day that I wasn't trying to enjoy my life. If I had too much to do, my mind would stay busy. I wouldn't have to deal with my problems. If I ran around never getting caught up, I could shut everyone out and not have time for anyone. If I didn't have friends, get involved in activities, and stayed to myself, I wouldn't get hurt. I began to shove everything inside and not release it. This business and isolation became a coping mechanism for me. It became as if all my sad emotions were connected to Peyton in some form, and I couldn't distinguish between causes for my emotions. I couldn't feel a normal sad emotion without it somehow connecting to Peyton.

Eventually, I learned that if I didn't heal, I would wake up one day and not even know who I was. If I made myself so busy, I would lose sight of myself. I needed to stop once in a while and if I didn't, my world would pass me by. I would never get to enjoy my life. I was forgetting what I needed and what made me happy. I knew some of these truths, but they seemed so far away to reach and unattainable. It was always as if my true happiness was just out of reach, I could visualize it but never catch up to it.

Somehow, along the way, I had lost who Peyton was. He was a joyful, silly child filled with so much love and happiness. He lit up a room whenever he entered it. He made all the other children laugh at his silly behavior. For so long, I had let myself remember the "dead" Peyton, a Peyton I had created from my grief. When memories of him came up, I couldn't enjoy the memory without ending it with the details and tragedy of his death. I knew I needed to remember him the way God had created him, not the way in which his life on earth had ended, but I could not seem to find my way out of the dark pit.

Isolation became a new normal for me. I would go out and engage with the world a few days a week for short periods of time, but I would always run home to where I believed my security was. My pain was so deep that I became so accustomed to it. When life became too much, I would sleep, and I began to sleep a lot. Sleep was the only escape I could find from my pain. My thoughts were too difficult to manage and control. But my pain was always waiting for me when I awoke. My escape became my prison.

I tried to immerse myself in my children. I do believe I was the best mom I could be; I gave myself and my time to them. I tried to make them a priority to the point I lost myself in them. When they weren't in school, I became "busy" with activities that made them happy, and in return, I would feel some happiness. As I look back though, I can see how I was always guarded. My walls that I had built were always around. I always carried around the "what if" and had the worst case scenario in my head, which would block me from experiencing the true happiness of the moment. I was always ready for crisis.

In the early days of my children's childhood, parenting them was easy. Their problems were easy to solve, and hugs and kisses made everything better. They were easy to love and take care of. For the most part, being a mother to them was an easy, joyful task. I served them with gladness. Since Peyton wasn't around, I tried to make their life the best possible. I wanted them to love their childhood and have fond memories of it. Being lost in them was a great escape until they grew older.

The pre-teen years brought difficulty, especially with my daughters. The problems were not so easy anymore. They became more complex and thought provoking. I began to realize just how much I had shielded my thoughts from pain. I became more aware of the walls I had built around me, and I knew that in order for me to be a good mom of older children, those walls would have to start coming down so I could help them with their own pains. I would have to allow myself to think painful thoughts and work out a solution with them. This may sound like a simple task but when you have been blocking thoughts of pain for years, it is difficult to retrain your brain that it is okay to have painful thoughts. I was being asked hard questions. This is when I slowly began to realize just how unaware I had been of a deep rooted pain in my life. I knew I had to start healing or my parenting and my children would suffer. I couldn't skate through my life anymore.

Chapter 8

Finally, Complete Healing

"The righteous cry, and the Lord heareth, and delivereth them out of all their troubles."
Psalm 34:17 (KJV)

In order to move forward, I had to let go. I had to understand that letting go of Peyton doesn't mean that I love him any less; it just means that I can focus on the life God had given me. I know now that it is okay not to cry each day. That it is okay if I go a week without thinking of Peyton. I need to allow myself to let Peyton go. He will always be a part of our family, but Peyton doesn't need all the time and energy I had been giving into grieving him. My family needs that time. I understand that my life will never be "normal" again; Peyton will always be missed. I will always feel like someone is missing; I will always be counting heads. I will have good days and bad days. I have decided that I do not want to live day to day dreading mundane tasks and stumbling through life without beauty, fun, joy, and legacy. I want to focus on God because He designed me. I have had to decide that I do not want to run and hide from my pain anymore. I know I will have my grief to deal with for the rest of my life. Each and every day I have a decision to make; I can choose to stay in my grief or choose to learn from this tragedy and become a better person because of my grief.

What I Have Learned

Having burdens in this life does not exempt me from experiencing further burdens. God will not shield me from all of life's difficulties;

it may be the opposite. God may allow difficulties because of what I have been through to mold me more into the person He wants me to be. He knows I need to be taught to be a witness in this world. He will allow struggle in my life to continue to transform me into who He wants me to be. God might use me in more ways and in more difficult situations because of what I have gone through. I can become a witness through my testimony. I need to welcome struggles because they show me that God believes in me. In my struggles, I am continually weak, so I need to allow God to be strong in my areas of weakness. If everything in life was good, I wouldn't feel the need to ask for God's help. If life were perfect, I wouldn't need to lean on God and wouldn't get to see His mighty hand at work.

When I empty myself, I create room for God to fill me. I remove the empty meaning that I can't allow (guilt, sin, hurts, or worry) to fill my heart. If I spend time on the negatives of life, they begin to inhabit me leaving no room for God. He implants a deep desire in all of us that is made just for Him—only He can fill it. We can search and search our whole lives looking for that which will make us feel happy and whole. This emptiness is the place where God should dwell: the place where God desires to dwell. He wants us to get to know Him.

I wish I could say that I chose Him to fill my empty void first. But for years before Peyton died, I was searching to find true happiness. I knew about God but I didn't have a relationship with Him. I was sure I had a time in my life where I made a commitment to Christ many years ago, but I never tried to *really* get to know *Him*. I knew all the stories about what He did through Himself and others, but I didn't realize that I wasn't getting to know God in my own world and the world around me. After Peyton died, I was forced to get to know God. I knew deep down that only He had all the answers. I began a quest for answers, and in doing so, I found the most amazing love that had been there all along. God wants us to be happy. He allows things to happen to us in our lives that might make us temporarily unhappy, but God knows the end result. He knows who we will become because of our pain. In time, God gives us what our heart truly desires. Most of the time, we ourselves don't even know what our own desires are. God knows what is best for us. He wants us to be dependent on Him, for this is how He designed us. He wants to turn our problems around and make us better because of them. What the evil one has intended for bad, God makes good.

We were not created for the pains of this world. God doesn't cause bad things to happen to us; fallen creation caused this. When Adam and Eve bit into the apple, sin was brought into this world. Humans had disobeyed God and the world He had created for them. In turn, God let us humans live with the consequences of sin. In order to create a relationship with us, God sent His Son, Jesus. Jesus had a human birth, walked on this Earth as human, died on the cross for our sins, and rose from the grave so we can live in eternity with Him. God loves us so much that He sent a piece of Himself, Jesus, to be human. The Great I Am lived among us with the same feelings, temptations, and heartaches. He put His divine status aside to be a human. He allowed Himself to be sacrificed in order to save us from ourselves. All we have to do in this life on earth is accept Him and His sacrifice. We are only on this Earth for a brief second, a dot on the grand line of eternity, but we will be with Jesus in Heaven forever.

The Devil only has access to us on Earth. This life right now is as bad as it gets if you're a Christian. The Devil wants to steal, kill, and destroy. He is the master of distractions. If the Evil One can make you believe that you don't have hope, he will keep you from God. The Evil One knows the Truth. He knows what power lies in the name of Jesus. He is just trying to blindfold this world so they don't believe. If we choose to believe, our lives will never be the same. When we are weak, He then has room to work. If we allow Him to work through us, we will be better for it.

We are not of this world. God made us for His world, the unseen world. This life will never make sense to us. The how and why might not ever be answered. I learned I just have to trust God, even when my whole body screams because of lies from this world. My life on earth will be a constant reminder of my sinful nature, my separation from God. I have to die to myself each day. I am not perfect; God is perfect. I am made perfect in God. The unnatural has happened. But Jesus conquered the grave. Jesus conquered my pain and suffering. In Him, I am whole. His kingdom is in me. I have more power than I can understand by the blood of Jesus. When I open up my life to Him, I give him permission to work through me and to use his power through me.

Keeping Peyton in the Family

Our children know who Peyton is: we show them pictures of him and tell them stories about him. We allow them to play with his special toys. We read his favorite books to them. We sing to them the songs he loved for us to sing. When we say our prayers each night, we ask God to give Peyton a hug and kiss for us. We keep him a part of our family. I have five children; Camden, Savannah, and Bristol know they have a brother in heaven keeping watch on them. They understand when I have bad days or cry unexpectedly that it is because I miss their brother. I try to include Peyton in special events or just ordinary days by mentioning him or adding something he would have enjoyed.

I have tried to be honest with them in a way that is age appropriate and doesn't make them fearful of death. As I was reading to Savannah one of Peyton's favorite books, she exclaimed out of the blue, "I love Peyton! I miss him!"

I always want them to have Peyton in their lives; I want them to know how much we love Peyton. How much he is missed. I want them to know that when faced with such horrible situations, God can help us overcome it.

As the children have grown older, we mention Peyton often. As crazy as it sounds, I still, fifteen years after Peyton's death, occasionally call Camden, Peyton by accident. It is a situation only a mother can understand. Just because Peyton is in Heaven doesn't mean that he is not still a part of my soul, a part of who I am as his mother.

I speak to my children openly about my pain and Peyton. As years tick by, they have come to understand that Peyton may be a small part of my pain now, but most of my tears just come from the difficulties of my life, which are partially from losing their brother. We often talk about who he would be or what he would have become. Savannah has always felt that she would have had a close bond with Peyton because their personalities are so similar.

As Camden has become older, he has brought friends into our lives that have created strong bonds with us. Many of his friends are older, a connection I believe he still has to Peyton. While I know no one will ever replace Peyton, God has planted special boys in our lives to show us the could-have-beens. We have embraced these friends, always in the back of our minds knowing this is how God is mending our hearts.

God Always Continues to Heal

Ten years after Peyton died, I began to experience some heart problems. I went to the emergency room and was admitted for observation. I was in the same hospital and close to the same room we were in the night before Peyton passed away. I didn't even realize the dates were almost the exact same also. A doctor walked into my room with his head held down and stood there. He spoke softly and said, "Do you remember me?" He could barely look me in the eyes. I told him I did not and was shocked when he said, "I am the doctor that treated Peyton the night before he died."

Jumping off my bed, I ran to give him a hug. He began to shake his head with it still held down and said, "I have held such guilt for not finding out what was wrong with your son. For ten years, I have not been able to work these dates because the reminders were too difficult. But this year, my wife told me it was time to put it behind me and work on his anniversary. When I came in, I saw your name on the board and I immediately called my wife and told her that 'Peyton's mom is here!' She told me to go to you but I had reservations about how you would feel about seeing me. She persuaded me to come in here."

I grabbed his arms and looked into his eyes that were full of sadness and pain and told him that me and my family had never blamed him nor did we ever think he should have found something. I told him that we always knew that God was in control and that if God had wanted us to find out what was wrong with Peyton, He would have allowed him is find it. I told him to drop his guilt and that there was no reason for him to carry it anymore, that he was a wonderful doctor and we saw that when he was treating Peyton.

I saw the pain lift from his body. He hugged me and I felt his sincere care. He thanked me and we cried. The door was open during all of this and as I looked into the halls, I noticed staff and nurses had gathered around. They knew what was happening and that the reason why he took off this weekend every year. Everyone was crying and smiling at what they had just witnessed. At this time, I told them, "Okay, I am better now! I know THIS was the reason God allowed me to have issues in order to have this divine encounter!" Of course, I couldn't be released and as I had felt, nothing was found at my overnight stay at the hospital. But I had a healing that penetrated deep into my heart.

One day I was walking along the beach by myself, collecting shells and trying to clear my head. A young boy ran up to me and began walking beside me. We began chatting. He was such a kind, sweet boy that felt familiar. I noticed his beautiful blue eyes. After a while, I heard his family and friends call to him, "Peyton!" I almost fell to my knees. As he ran off saying goodbye, I felt God's presence. This boy was around the same age Peyton would have been now. It was just another precious wink from God.

Years after Peyton died, we wanted to build a house and be by the water. Originally, we were in a house that was difficult to enter after Peyton died, but we began to not want to leave the home because that was where all of our memories were. I especially didn't want to leave our "Peyton Tree" a tree Peyton always climbed.

When we put our house on the market, I noticed the "Peyton tree" didn't look so good, a huge Mimosa tree. A few days later it was dead! God revealed to my heart that it was time to move and not to attach myself to things of this world. While our new house was being built, I walked around it and noticed that all the insulation was stamped October 19, the day Peyton had died. Peyton was always going to be with us no matter where we were.

The day I moved the last bit of stuff from the home, it was difficult. I had saved the "special" boxes of Peyton's things to go in my car because I didn't trust anyone else with them. As I was packing them in, a bird flew in my jeep and just sat on my dashboard while I was loading them up. It was a wink from God in Heaven letting me know He was always with me in the difficult times.

A New Season of Life

As the seasons change each year into fall, the weather begins to cool, and Halloween decorations come out, I find that the reminders of the most terrifying day of my life will always be with me. I understand that this will always be no matter how many years have passed. I also know that it does not have to control my life anymore. Many of the horrible details sneak into my memory when reminders hit my senses and make me unconsciously aware that I still hold that grief, and I have to give it right back to God.

I have to incorporate my son's death into every new detail of my life. His death and my survival of his death is a huge part of who I am and what my story is. Meeting new people, beginning new hobbies, whatever new adventure God has in store for me, I have to bring the reality of my son's death with me and what that looks like is different for each season. I will forever grieve my son and have a hole in my heart for him. While I still hold the pain, God is holding me. And I now have the gracious pleasure of handing it back to God. He sent Jesus to do that that for us. I cannot bring Peyton back. He isn't in my past anymore but in my future. I have the hope that he is in heaven awaiting my arrival. The glorious reward at the end of a life well lived.

For now, I want to live to serve the Lord. I want to be a reminder that while this life may be extremely difficult, we don't have to live with the pain alone. I want to live a better life because of my son's death. I know God makes beauty out of ashes. I know pain. I know healing. I have stopped reminding myself of the difficult things I have been through and reminding myself of what God has brought me through. If I carry this pain of losing Peyton all the time, it doesn't allow me to show that I miss him any more, it just shows that I am trusting God less. I am trusting God through my

Finally, Complete Healing

pain, and He has shown up in greater ways than I could have ever imagined to heal my heart. This life is short but Heaven is eternal.

Journal Entries

Jan. 2, 2009

Camden said he wants to have his birthday party in Heaven. Then, he said he wants to spend "one night" up in Heaven. We began started talking about things in Heaven. When I told him there were rats in Heaven, he said, "No, I didn't see them." He paused for a while and said, "Oh yeah, I did but I didn't know they were rats. They change colors, Purple, yellow, blue whatever color you want them to be, God will change them for you!"

Aug.17, 2009

I woke up last night and found Savannah's little lamb lying face down on my chest. I thought, Well, maybe Camey had her in the bed with us. I put her on the floor and rolled over and felt Camey and he had Savannah's big lamb face down on his chest as he slept. A gift from Heaven!

June 5, 2009

Fuel my fire, Father God. Ignite a fire in me. Make my voice loud. Help me make this life easier and happier for others. Help me bring people into Your kingdom.

Feb. 7, 2011

Another birthday is coming up, and he would be turning five. I know he's up in heaven watching, waiting for me to arrive. But I still can't help but miss him wishing he were here; I'm still asking why this happened—

so many things are still unclear. I miss his contagious laugher, his presence in our home. At times I grieve so badly not accepting that he's gone. I still feel guilty when I laugh or share a simple smile. I know its what he wants of me but it's only been a short while. I have such a strong urge to share Jesus with others. I'm asking that others learn from my son's death that time is fleeting, so cherish every breath. I pray that others know Jesus because He's up there waiting. When their time has come to leave this Earth, I want them to meet my Peyton!

Sept. 11, 2013

I struggle. Most days I am not good at being who God created me to be. Some days everything goes wrong. More days than not, I spill things, break things, lock myself out, lose my keys or phone. I feel a wreck inside. Somedays, I just want to be all alone for a short while. Then I often feel like a failure. The whys, what ifs, and hows, crowd my mind.

I am blessed! Look at what I have overcome. Look around my life and see all that is good. I am choosing to listen to God and not the lies of the devil. I may fail, but I will always rise.

Sept. 12, 2013

Before Peyton died, I was carefree. Whatever happened, I would respond with, Okay, let it roll off my back, be easy going, no worries. Now I have greatly changed; I know I had to and should in some ways, but Father God, I want the laid-back personality trait to come back. When little things go wrong, I want to laugh about them and let them roll off and not stress about them. I want to relax and enjoy life. I want the old me, whom I loved, to come back. I trust in you, Lord. Teach me how to be worry-free and how to relax. Teach me how to open my heart. Teach me how to roll with life with ease. I do not want to be uptight. I do not want to be closed, sealed off, judgmental nor too cautions. I want to walk by faith with my eyes always on You!

Jan. 19, 2014

As I sit here listening to the birds, I hear a familiar song from a bird that intrigues me. I remember hearing the song only a few years ago for the first time ever. I heard it just a few times that first year during migration. Now, I have been hearing it more and more often. As I sit today, I hear it but do not get as excited as I once did to hear it. It was once unusual and different, now it has become common. Yes, I still think the bird has the prettiest song but I have become used to its uniqueness. I do not want to become this way. I want to hear something as if it is my very first time. I want to see things as if my eyes have never seen anything like it before. I want to experience things like they are brand new. I don't want to get cold to God's hand. Nor do I wish to become cold and stale to the love I have for others. I do not want to take things for granted and get used to how things are. I know it can all change in an instant!

July 2014

I had a dream last night. I was somewhere familiar

and all of these people started coming up to me and greeting me. Lots of people came and began to surround me. I had this amazing feeling of excitement and joy as if I were at a party. I saw people I knew I recognized but as I think about it, I can't tell you who anyone was. Someone handed me a folded piece of paper. I opened it and began reading it aloud. Suddenly, it hit me: I was reading the letter that I put in the casket with Peyton! I had forgotten I had even written this letter, but the words I had written down in those horrific moments right after Peyton died were now being read by me in this moment. As I began to understand what I had just read, I said, "He's here?!"

I realized I was in Heaven. The crowd opened up, and everyone was cheering and crying with excitement. I knew I was about to see Peyton again.

Nov. 19, 2014

Once we allow a thought, an idea to entertain us, it starts to have control over us. We begin to see it around a little more, and it begins to bleed into our character. It begins to affect our outlook on life, our perception of things.

If this thought is negative, it can cause a snowball effect in our lives. We begin to compromise. The line between black and white starts to add shades of grey where we are unaware. A new dimension is opened. We start seeing thing in a new light (or darkness), and a false reality begins to cloud our clarity of how things should be. We begin to fall but don't even notice the depths to which we are sinking. If we don't have a compass, a light to guide our path, we may never realize nor understand just how far we have fallen. Then we don't recognize our own reflections. We aren't who we once were and we feel empty. We have created a void in our life so great that we begin to drown for a lack of substance in our lives. We realize the compromise has stolen our joy and peace. We no longer live on a stable foundation. Anything can knock us over; a hint of wind knock us off course.

If we are blessed by mercy from Heaven, we understand the magnitude of our situation and it only has one savior. If we cast all of our imperfections and our misunderstood conceptions of happiness on Him—and only Him—to become our guiding light, we can escape our own prison. He becomes our life raft, and we release all unnecessary things that have begun attach themselves to us and weigh us down. It is at that moment when we start to understand true forgiveness. We see how heavy our sins have been and how blindingly they have guided us. There is always hope. We have to become so uncomfortable with the lies and distractions of this world that Christ Jesus if the only thing that satisfies. If we look to anything else, we will forever be searching to full a bottomless void.

Jan. 22, 2015

I will not let others' opinions change what I believe. I am grounded in my faith and know what I believe. God will show me my path. God will make a way. If God is for me who can come against me? God runs my life. God is in control. I am capable. I am able. I am a strong, beautiful, and conquering woman. I make ripples wherever I go. I make a difference in this world. I am fearfully made, and I am loved!

Feb. 27, 2015

I am created to be a blessing to others. If I do not, I will suffer. I am called to speak and to lead. If I sacrifice my time just for my family and those close to me and avoid God's work, I will run on empty. I need the strength that God gives to me when I obey Him. If I am not being used by God, my overflow (to the ones I love) will run dry and stale. If something comes up that God needs me to do, I have to follow. I am HIS! We are not here on this planet just for us. I have to do my part. I am going to have to let go of some things in my life. I am going to let go of my selfish ways.

March 10, 2015

As I am sitting in my quiet closet, it isn't very quiet! The kids are home from school today because we are sick. I am reading my Bible and trying to concentrate on the Word, but I hear cartoons, computer, and Xbox. I try to quieten my soul despite the noises. As I sit with my eyes closed, I begin to hear my radio playing in the distance. I concentrate on it. The other noises begin to be drowned out by the worship music. God spoke to me and said, "So is the way with My voice."

I get so wrapped up in the static of life that I allow it to drown out the voice of God. I have been in a struggle for a while. My faith is being tested. I am being tempted in different directions. My mind feels crazy. Being who I want to be (who God wants me to be) takes work! At this point, my battle is mental and spiritual. Give me Your strength, and truth, Heavenly Father.

May 17, 2016

Always be on the lookout for Jesus as He were someone you loved in your past that might bump into you today. Live every minute of the day as if He were to pop in at any time for an unannounced visit. Never be living a life you wouldn't want the whole world to see if it were to be broadcasted on national TV. Expect the unexpected. Be prepared and live like tomorrow will never come and that this moment is your only chance.

Jan. 7, 2017

This morning, I was reading about Martha telling Jesus that Lazarus was dead and buried. If He had only come four days before when they sent for Him before Lazarus died, He could have saved him. Martha knew He could have prevented his death but never believed that Jesus could raise him after death was final.

My faith has had limits. I believed that my healing could only reach a certain point, that my grief would always remain. But that belief is limiting my faith in God. As I grow in Christ and my faith grows, my grief should lessen. God wants to restore to me what I have lost. But will I let Him? Do I believe that I am letting a little more of Peyton disappear if I allow this? And if it is, why is that so difficult?

There is this cold, black hole in my life. A place I rarely

i Hope for Heaven

try to go. I may observe from afar but go back into the abyss, I get lost. Is that normal? Is that healthy? What haven't I let go of? Do I blame my problem on everything else when in actuality it is the reality of losing my son that I hold on to so tight that it cripples my everyday life? Do I subconsciously use my grief as a crutch? If so, how do I release it?

Nov. 9, 2021

If I hold onto this pain any longer, I am doing God a disservice. He had a bigger plan when he allowed Peyton to die. I have to not only trust Him in this knowledge, but I must also live it out now. It is time. Fifteen years of allowing deep pain to cripple me must stop. I have to allow God to heal my whole heart. I can't keep taking my pain back from Him.

"On Peyton's Grave"—Jennifer Ingram

We miss you so much our precious angel boy
You filled our lives with such happiness and joy.
God fulfilled His plan for you and your life here on Earth.
He had His hand on you with purpose ever since your birth.
On the day you left us, you did not go alone
For pieces of our hearts you took the day God called you home.
We treasure our memories and, in our hearts, they will endure
For we know now you're not in our past but in our future.
Today, the Lord will carry us and give us His grace
Until the day we are with you kissing your glorious face!

How to Help Someone Who Is Grieving

I learned to not compare my grief with someone. We are created very differently; therefore, we grieve very differently. What might work for some, will not for others. Males and females grieve very differently. I cannot say I understand what all grieving mothers go through. I know how it feels to have a son die, but I could never understand someone else's grief. I have had a hard enough time understanding my own.

The best thing you can do for a friend or loved one who is grieving is give them your presence. Just sit with them and listen if they need to talk. Two of my friends called me every day for a year after Peyton died. This annoyed me at times because I did not feel like talking, but upon looking back, their phone calls were exactly what I needed. Sometimes, I would answer and talk, other times I couldn't. They would still call and leave me a sweet message that let me know that they cared. Those reminders helped me more than words can express. I could trust that a call would come from them each day, which gave me comfort to know I was loved even if I never spoke.

Another thing you can do is remember their child's birthday and the day they entered Heaven. This was huge for me. It hurts my feelings worse if my close friends and loved ones forget Peyton's birthday than if they forget my birthday. A lot of people think that it would be too difficult for the bereaved if someone called and brought up their child's birthday. But the grieving mom knows this date. I know for me, even if I had no clue what the current date was, I always knew when Peyton's birthday rolled around. It is a connection a mom feels deep inside. Give a call, leave a message, or send a card, but most importantly, remember!

You can also get her a book, music or something she used to enjoy to bring her comfort. It is just the thought that goes a long way. Mail her a card. I always looked forward to checking my mail. Buy her a journal. I found that writing was very beneficial to my healing process.

The biggest comfort is to give your time, in any way. Help around the house. Cook her dinner. Stop by and say hey. Check in with her from time to time. Let her know that she is not alone.

Now that I am on the healing side of grief, I often get calls from people who are friends with someone who just lost a child. I am more than willing to call, write, and send the items that comforted me during my difficult season. If you have a friend or know of a friend's friend who has come through this type of grief, contact this grieving mom. It helped me to know about someone who had also lost a child and to see them living and doing okay in life after a period of time. They understood more than anyone else could. Just being in the presence of another mom who had lost a child was comfort enough. No words even had to be spoken.

Yielding to Emergency Vehicles

As I rode in the Ambulance in a frantic race to get to the hospital, I saw a number of drivers who had no clue what to do with the ambulance approaching. In my everyday driving today, I still see this problem. Each state has different laws about what you should do if an ambulance approaches. Most states are relatively the same.

» Try to see which direction the sound is coming from and where it is headed.
» You must yield to emergency vehicles if they are using a siren and flashing lights.
» If the emergency vehicle is approaching from behind, pull off the road, but not in an intersection. Go through the intersection and once safely through, pull to the right until the emergency vehicle has passed.
» If a median separates you from the emergency vehicle, you do not have to pull over.
» If an emergency vehicle approaches from the opposite direction, slow down and try to pull over. If cars are behind you do not put on brakes and quickly move over, gently slow down and, if needed, pull over.
» If you see an ambulance approaching when are stopped at a red light, watch where the ambulance is heading. If it is coming up behind you, pull to one side, in the median if you have to, allowing the EMS to pass.
» Do not follow more than 500 feet behind an emergency vehicle with sirens and lights on.
» Remember that seconds are critical to the person in the emergency vehicle. Seconds can save a life.

Confirmations and Dates

- February 7, 2003 - Peyton is born
- February 2, 2005 - Camden is born
- October 19, 2006 - Peyton dies
- March 22, 2007 - Camden talks about Peyton's house in Heaven with big gates, pretty water, and fireworks. Camden is two years and one month old.
- Between May 5th and 15th, 2007 - I had my miscarriage at twelve weeks. Camden told me that Peyton had a baby. The next day, Camden asks me what my baby's name is. Camden is two years and three months old.
- August 10, 2007 - Camden tells me about Peyton doing "boingeys" in heaven. Also, Peyton "talks God to me." This vision is confirmed by my sister telling me she was in the middle of prayer asking God what Peyton was doing in Heaven when I called telling her about what Peyton was doing. Camden is two and a half.
- August 30, 2007 – I find out I am pregnant with Savannah. Camden tells us about the baby before we tell him or anyone else.
- Oct. 28, 2007 - Camden tells me that God makes Peyton giggle. It is confirmed by my parents' friend in a vision. Camden is two years and eight months old.
- May 7, 2008 - Savannah is born.
- May 12, 2008 - I receive a hug from heaven. Camden confirms that Peyton was supposed to give me a "hug from heaven." Camden is three years old.
- July 17, 2008 - Gena has her vision of Peyton on my birthday. This vision is confirmed by her telling me what he was

Confirmations and Dates

wearing, which were the same clothes he had on when he died.
- January 6, 2010 - Bristol is born.
- 2015 - I make notes of all of the sevens in our family and realize that there are a lot. God reminds me of when He told me: "Your family isn't complete yet." Putting down the seven years that separated Peyton and Bristol's birth, I understand that Bristol completed our family!

CPSIA information can be obtained
at www.ICGtesting.com
Printed in the USA
BVHW031123300922
648381BV00013B/435